T0104029

PASSING THROUGH

Book Number 4

David Marshall

Order this book online at www.trafford.com
or email orders@trafford.com

Most Trafford titles are also available at major online book retailers.

© Copyright 2015 David Marshall.
All rights reserved. No part of this publication may be reproduced,
stored in a retrieval system, or transmitted, in any form or by
any means, electronic, mechanical, photocopying, recording, or
otherwise, without the written prior permission of the author.

Print information available on the last page.

ISBN: 978-1-4907-6511-2 (sc)
ISBN: 978-1-4907-6510-5 (e)

Because of the dynamic nature of the Internet, any web addresses or links contained in
this book may have changed since publication and may no longer be valid. The views
expressed in this work are solely those of the author and do not necessarily reflect the
views of the publisher, and the publisher hereby disclaims any responsibility for them.

Any people depicted in stock imagery provided by Thinkstock are models,
and such images are being used for illustrative purposes only.
Certain stock imagery © Thinkstock.

Trafford rev. 09/22/2015

Trafford PUBLISHING® www.trafford.com
North America & international
toll-free: 1 888 232 4444 (USA & Canada)
fax: 812 355 4082

Repent.

To feeling sorry for my sin, to feeling such regret over my action intention, as to change one mind about my life story repentant.

I wrote my life story Passing Through book one, too, and three it was true, but, I left out something out, I dint put in my book, about when my Grandmother, she was so good, but I dint put in my book and after I left school and got marry to Barbara Jean, and came to Chicago, Ill with my wife, and got a job as dish washer, at Nelsen Cafeteria, my father in law he got the job, his name David STALLWORD.

Date 06-30-2015

CHARTER 1

*I*t was about my age 8 years old, that is a guy in Brewton, Alabama his name is Wilson London, he was my buddy, his mother they was seller a bike, I want to buy, I never had no bike. My Grandmother she had a cessiro, a piece of furniture, she put her money in the cessiro, I knew it keep, I sat by the cessiro, I fish out $20.00 and put it in my pocket, I left then I went to Wilson London and paid for $10.00 the bike. I said, I own a bike, I was so happy, I got a bike, I was wrong Grandmother, I am sorry.

Just like someone said that, the first book Passing Through talk about David STALLWORD my father in law, that take money while Nelsen Cafeteria at work, he got me the job, I don't say that we don't ask or talk about, but I saw him take money, but we don't talk about, but I got mind. And loner money quarter for dollar loner shark. Now I got it over, now I was so worry that, I dint put in my book of Passing Through, now I can finish my book that I can leave behind after I pass on.

But, be four I left from Brewton, Alabama the last time be four I, left I brought down my birthday and brought the book the peoples did to me. If Jackie my daughter if she need me, I will be back. If you don't want me or see anymore, my step father he said David lee, I guess you want be back anymore, I don't want to say because I love my step father, I said no.

Now I call Jackie my Daughter to put in advertise to put in the new paper, in Brewton Stander, to wrote my advertise how to go and sent the money to pay for it, Passing Through I did that, I sent 50 copy books to arise to my stepfather address to arise for me, Jackie call me that the ad was in the paper, I ask Jackie to send me to 5 copy for me, she did. I got the ad in my paper they put it the Obituary secession, I said that was ok I would straighten out later, after I get to Brewton but I forgot it.

You see Brenda Crosby, Fred and Jackie there was just baby, Jackie she was just born, Fred he was just walking, I dint do by my family, I was drinking Brenda she ran down stair to get away from me, her mother she got tried, she got a bus she got her Daughter and went back and went back home, I let them down. I dint do the right thing by them, I had women I had all them now I want them back my family, but I want them back, I am so sorry that I dint do the right thing by my family. But if her mother Brenda, and if I dint break up, she would not have those so beautiful girls, lady. I marry Brenda Crosby, I still love Brenda Crosby.

I meet Abby and her brother down the street, on the 48th street I was start to go with her, I got a job with Burnside steel founder, I was taken the bus to work, under the train track the white people wrote no nigger loud. We had to get a ride with some other peoples, until to take another bus at 93st to get to work, I was working to 3pm to 11pm, Joe Pitt I was going with his old lady Core her name he found out, Abby I was going to work, Joe Pitt he was going to see Abby going with her, because Core I was going with her, Joe and Core they was staying too house from me.

David Douglas, Abby and Barbara Jean Marshall we broke up, she came to start living with me to see if try to make it, I was living over the Crosby dad store, David Douglas, and Abby she was going with her spouse with Abby and David Douglas going with to gather, then Barbara found out she move out she move back to Maywood, Ill. I got off work and came home, I found out Abby sister line back on the couch, I snap, I said get out Abby and her sister they ran off, I said dint need them. I came up to the week end I went to the Castle Rock Lounge to get a beer.

Then I meet Mary William, She was in the Castle Rock Lounge Abby and was with other peoples, I saw Mary she was to find, she had Chinese eyes I could not keep my eyes on her, I said that I was going to get her, I did. Not right then but I got her later on I marry her. Until we went to Brewton, Alabama to see Jackie my Daughter, after we arise I want to see my Daughter Jackie, I told Mary that come on I want to see Jackie, then all hell broken out she and I had a fright, I went to see Jackie, after I came back I ask where is Mary, they said left, I was staying with ZEB. We look for Mary no Mary.

We told the Police I gave her futurity how she look, they said that they was going to keep her eye on, I said thank you, we went to my step Farther and sit around I was worry about Mary, I said where are Mary went she don't know anybody in Brewton where are she at, I was worry about her. My step Farther he said, David why don't you relax why don't you call home tomorrow, call home she may be at home relax yourself, I said than you daddy.

That morning I call home Mary she answer the phone, I was relieve we talk, I said that she would see her at home, she said ok we hung up the phone, I told my step Farther Mary she was at home, he said that she thought was going home, after Jackie I saw her and I got home to back to Chicago, I said that Jackie is my child, I don't want to see Brenda, I ask her did you want to go but we fright, Jackie is my child did I going to all the way I dint see her, no way, Mary she pass.

A best friend of mind name Doll John and I was in the Club Protection, it was crower Doll John he was my partner, he was a bus driver, as all peoples coming in there Doll he made a bet, that the next lady coming in and sit down by me or I, I said how much he said $5.00, Doll he said you bet.

About a ½ hour a woman came in she look around then she said, to me is that seat vacant? I said no you can have it, she sit down, Doll he said you mother fuck. She is long hair she is find, she order a dink, bartender she was going to pay for the drink, I said I got it I pay for the drink, then I start a commission, I ask her name, she said Mary William, I said hum, she said why? I said Mary William hum, later on we got a house, we start living to gather, when we was off the job, all the kids we got to stay in bed to watch the TV, at 91st Morgan.

We stay almost 3 years we was having find I love Mary and the kids, my buddy she induce me to cousin Little John, Leaner, she was to find I start to go with her that was to do something, Leaner she came to put note in the mail slots, Jr. Mary son he inspect the note he gave the note to me, he dint want to mother to see it. When Leaner I see her why you did that put a note in my mail slots why, she said that I want to see you, don't do that anymore, Leaner she keep on put notes in the mail slots, then we break up I move out, to apartment over on 91ˢᵗ and Ashland, then I meet Gil's Lounge down the Street.

After I went down to Gil's Tiete Lounge, I order a beer and I was sitting on the bar stool, then I walk to the juke box, I punch some records then I sit back down, to listen to hear the music then I meet Gil's, he brought me a beer then Gil's we was talking, then Gil's he said that he told me that he had a cleaner, I said o yes, he told me where it was at, I said ok then he had a phone call, Gil's he had to go to the cleaner.

He ask me to go with to see where the cleaner was at, I went to him. After Gil's and I was going as we was knowing all the time, the boiler was out, the boiler man I meet him his name was Jessie, I said hi, the next I meet his son Pat, I said hi, then his Daughters he had 5 Daughter, I meet them all the family that was working, after Gil's we finish, we was going to leave going back to the lounge, I told them see you I was going to see you soon, then we left.

After then Gil's and I we came to be the best friend. Then Mary William 2ⁿᵈ we got a divorce, then I meet Sally at Roy and Jimmy Lounge, Sally, Roy and Jimmy they are friend. On Saturday we was off work, we all about 10 friend we put 2 table to gather, we all had fun that Saturday, Sally she and I we got along to gather, she start living to gather, Sally she had old man they could not get along to gather, she went to Brewton, Alabama to gather, I had a vacation and Sally she also was on vacation too.

Then I said that why don't we going to go someplace that we never being before, she said where? Then I went to go and fill up the car, then I drove to 65 highway we only with the clothes on our back, she ask where are we going, I said just ride, first Indianapolis she ask again where are you going, I said just ride Kentucky we got gas use the rest room then we, just we are just ride.

Then we went to Tennessee, after we got throw Birmingham we saw the iron man, Sally she said the iron man he standing on the Mountain, she said that someone said the iron man hum, we keep on driving until we came up to Montgomery, but I dint tell her where we was going until I park in front my step farther house we got about 4: am we got out.

Then I knock on the window, he said how is it, I said David Marshall your son, someone is playing with me, he open the door, I was standing with Sally it was your son he said you could have call, I said that I came to have a drink we are leaving out, we drank all the alcohol until the state store open, then I will buy some more then I will replace your, then I will get some sleep, then I am leaving out.

My step father he gave Sally a plant to take back, I dig up a bush out from the ground, to put in trunk then to tie the trunk, then the state store it was open, we went to the state store and replace the alcohol for daddy, I replace pay ½ gallon each of alcohol for daddy 3 ½ gallon each and a case a beer, then we had a ball, then I got some sleep.

After I woke my daddy he put the plant the trunk, in the car and tie the trunk, I got ready to leaving ZEB. He said that you all you going to have a drank you are leaving, I said that all I was going to have a drink, now I am going to leaving going back home, it was the time about 6:pm, I would call you after we get home, we left going back.

After we got home I call daddy that I am at home, daddy he said he was going to tell them you got home safe, I said ok, then Sally she went to her home, I went to Gil's lounge, Gil's he ask where you been, I said was in Brewton, Alabama.

Then I meet Terry she was working at 3 doors by Gil's Lounge, we all was in Gil's Lounge having good time, I was Lee Berry I said that do you to be talking with that lady on the bar, Lee Berry he said that the small one we dint know there name, but Lee Berry he had old lady she is going to take his ride, I said that I don't like no big fat lady, I want the small woman I got her. Later on I was talking to her at Gil's Lounge, I bout her a drink we was talking she was at work, she said she was going she was be back, then she left I was still looking at her, then Jake he was the Mechanic the next door, then told Jake I love that woman, he ask what who, I said Terry.

Jake he said you got they wedding ring then he left, Jake they all way fighting but they are friends, after Terry and I got tight because I marry her, after we got a Divorce, we and her she we got the best friend after.

Janice, I was looking for another Lady her name Janice, I was looking for was at Ruth Lounge on 89th on Loomis, but another Janice I marry her but she was good. Richard we was at the wedding the start, then Richard he said you can walk away and forget that wedding, I said no because if I gave my word, Richard and he said again you can walk away we want get mad, I said still my word are my word bond, we got marry her Janice Marshall for hell.

MY play sister Bobby she came to Gil's she ask do you want to go with her to Bingo, I said no way I don't play Bingo, she said no I want to see a woman, that she work at the nursing home her name is Jackie Child she is single, I said ok, I meet Jackie Child we and got along well, I start to working with the nursing home. Then I start staying with Jackie Childs, I went to go Kentucky and I meet the Family, we had fun I went to Brewton, Alabama, to my Daughter wedding. Jackie Childs I was a common Law marriage.

Then I meet Bernice Jordan. Bobby she was a cousin of Bernice Jordan, I wrote a letter every day to her, after then I marry Bernice Jordan Marshall, after then I move to Las Vegas, NV. She dint want me because, I marry Bernice because the man he make Jealous, I move to many time and came back, until 4 time back and forth, until I meet Robert and Joyce Thomas my cousin.

Robert and Joyce Thomas we move me, because I was tired I had move about every 3 month, I was so tried then I move in the Loma Vista apartment homes, cross Martin l. king and Cheyenne Ave, after I had to new release I sign it, Joyce she said why don't you, go to Martin I. king Blvd and Lake Mead and get apartment, yes ok then I went there and got apartment, I came back to the Lease office to Loma Vista I told and ex plan to the office they tow up the new Lease, I did what Joyce did I move in, I been staying living at M. l. k. Blvd. build #3 and apartment 152, I wrote 3 books and still writing.

CHAPTER 2

$\mathcal{M}$y Grandmother please forgive me for I took the money, I need to forgive me Grandmother, please to Grandmother forgive me I have to 3 time to forgive me, I was not angel. As I would say that I am so sorry that I did to you, to the woman I am so sorry that they did to them, I had so many.

God, he made man to his image with him, I see God and Jesus in the mirror. I know man don't like me, but I don't care. But I respect man and hope respect me, I feel show honor or esteem to man, but I want be no yes man. If I know something I will talk about it, but if I don't know something to talk about I short my mouth and listen, but I want be no yes man.

But a woman, a woman one day said to me that, the ways of a woman is never known, they love to keep a man living in a fancy or a woman, but that is ok by a man, because his woman she is his pet, just love her. We man try to keep her woman happy, bring her candy, flower, kiss her and make love to her, then after a man going then she will go to see another man, after the man come back, she get back as nothing as anything wrong, someone else was banging her woman.

One day I was going to mom. Evelyn after her son he pass on, I went to the funeral, be four he was sitting on a rock he was talking to Mr. Brown, I was walking around, I was walking to my health medical, I said to high to little Richard mom. Evelyn son and Mr. Brown, then I keep on walking little Richard he told her mom, David don't mistreat him because he would be at her side, after he was pass don't mistreat him, I said that I want do that, we was going to the Doctor appointment, we went to the Doctor office, after we left the Doctor office I ask did she need to go anywhere else, she said no then we went home, she got out my truck she went to the house, I left going back home.

On the August about 17, 2012 John Marshall my son he call me, he said call my brother in Pensacola, Fl. I call Jackie my daughter, what wrong with ZEBEDEE, she was in the hospital, I ask was it bad, Jackie said he don't make it, then I call Angelia my niece she answer the phone, she said it was Angelia she said high uncle David lee how are you doing, I said ok then we talk then she gave my brother the phone, I ask how are you doing, he said he was doing find, I told him you not to good he was in the hospital, he was doing find then he gave the phone to Angelia, I said he don't want to talk, Angelia she said well, I told Angelia if he don't get no better I would come to Brewton, she said ok then we hung up the phone.

Later on John Marshall my son he call me, that ZEBEDEE your brother he pass, I said to me he dint to make no mend to me, that what he did to me I said that is ok, he took to his grave but I was going to his funeral. Then I ask Joyce Thomas my cousin, my brother ZEBEDEE he pass in Alabama to get my ticket, Joyce she did then Robert and Joyce Thomas they, took me to the Airport. I went down to Brewton, Alabama,

I arise Jackie and Angelia she was waving to me, we huge them someone Angela ask uncle David lee, do you know that woman, I said no Jackie she said Anger your X brother in law, I huge her I could not I get enough, I said Anger, Anger you looking good, she you are looking good to then we Mr. Jones, they got a renter car then after we got some coffee, then we left then we going back to Brewton, Alabama.

When Jackie and I got to her house, we went into the house I put it the luggage down, I saw my Grandson I spoke then I shake his hand, then how you doing, he said find. then Jackie she said come on we are going to mom house, we went to Brenda house I saw her kids that is not kids anymore, I huge them then I saw her Brenda Grandkids, I said high to them.

After Mr. Jones, Angelia and Anger her mother, then we went to Mary Carol BRYER house Zebedee wife, then I saw Dee, Dee Bayer I huge him then I shake his hand, he said that I haft seen you alone time, I smile along time I said after we was drink some beer, when Zebedee he got mad he dint want to drank, we went to a case a beer, then we sit around and talk to each other, he was smiling he said uncle David lee I haven, I am at home.

After we sit around talking then we decide to go Brenda house, so we went to Brenda house all of them, I saw Mary Stallworth, Eddie Stallworth sister I had a cress on her, then Matt he are John Marshall my son cousin we talk, then the house was full drink beer and wine, Angelia mother she was drinking wine, I was drinking some beer and wine Dee, Dee we had a good time, Angelia she stay with Brenda until he old man Mr. Jones he came back until they was staying in the hotel, her mother she staying with Jackie with us.

After that morning we woke up we said good morning, we all went to Brenda house because James my cousin, James Smith he was cooking we all went to breakfast, James he call me a lie because I was going to move back to Brewton, but I decide not to move, I call Zebedee I told him that I decided not to move back, because Jackie her aunt she and we talk to her, she that David lee you are not going to live long, people don't live long there is know where to go, like VEGAS you have plenty to go to see, she is right then I decide not to move, James he could have told me, I said Zebedee he told him.

Then it was to see the body, before the funeral it was Dee, Dee, Mr. Jones, Angelia and I went to see the body, I sing the register, I look at my brother body it was sleeping and com, I said why, why I said why you can stand me why? You was my brother why, you would take to the grave that to say to sorry, about how to treat me, but you are my brother I love you, I am going now to say, I want to say, I am sorry that you treat me, I am so sorry. Then we left to have the wake, now I was relax that I repent for me, I love my brother.

At the wake for my brother I meet the kids. Then Dee, Dee he ask them did you know them, I said no, the older child he said Zebedee the 4th I dint know it, I huge him then the small child I meet him I huge him, the little girl I took her hand I said high to her, then I meet Dee, Dee wife her name is Shana BRYE, I said that high she was beautiful, Dee, Dee he was so proud I know he was smiling, the kids we talk to them, I told them that if I see them no matter where, I told them if I see them I will recognize you or me, I will recognize you or me, we are family I said ok. Then they said ok.

Then Jackie, Mamma Ruth cousin and I was talking, 2 lady came in Jackie she said why did they got some nerve,

why they came to wake, I ask who was they, Jackie she said
Zebedee her Daughter so call her Daughter, I said I will see I
went to the funeral home to see, I ask them to induce them,
I am Zebedee brother David lee Marshall, they said they was
coming out from Montgomery, Alabama to VEW the body,
we talk then we took some picture, then we left the wake was
over to the funeral.

We woke up to put my brother in the ground, we got dress
and went to Mary Carol home, to take the funeral family
car, to take the church we line up and walk into that church
and sit down, the castle it was close, Jackie she read Passing
Through that I wrote, Angelia her old man Mr. jones he was
the preacher, that the preach the funeral, he could preach,
then we left to the grave site, we put Zebedee in the ground,
after the final over I saw Jack Rankin, Otis Red mon, Jackie
Gully her sister she said that Jackie I was going to tell her
that I saw her, I saw Dog, Mary Carol brother and so many I
dint see.

They we ate I meet some other BRYE brother that I dint
know, like HUZELL BRYE I meet him but I forget the other
he was from Every Green, Alabama, another guy he was
talking to me, he said that he was the last one living for him,
I told him that the BRYE family I don't have any more, but
the Crosby family I have three other brother and one sister
left. Then we eat we went to Mary Carol home, Shana Dee,
Dee Husband I took some picture then they was leaving going
back to NC, I said that I would see the kids, I will see you
soon, then they left Dee, Dee he stay in Brewton, I said to
Jackie I was going to take my monkey suit take it off, then we
left going home to take my suit off.

Obituary

In loving Memory Zebedee BRYE Jr. sunrise January 21, 1940, sunset August 23, 2012, service Friday, August 31, 2012, 11:00 am, Second Saint Siloam MBC 290 East Street, Brewton, AL 364226 Rev. Willie Blue, Pastor. Officiating: Arthur C. Jones Jr. Pastor, First Baptist Tabernacle Church,

Order of celebration Processional Scripture Old and new Testament Prayer, Clergy &Family Pastor Willie J. Blue Second Saint Siloam MBC Minister, Solo card/ Acknowledgements/Resolutions Mamie Hamilton Obituary Shana BRYE Daughter-in-Law, Reflections (2 minutes please) Tributes David Lee, Brother, Angelia BRYE-Jones, Daughter, Zebedee BRYE III, son, Song Message of Life Arthur Jones Jr. Pastor First Baptist Tabernacle Church Sacramento, California. Active Pallbearers Kenny Campbell, James Smith, Henry Palmer, Samford Johnson Jr. Joe Watson, Aaron Nicholson,

Then I meet Shana BRYE her Father he is cool and the kids they is cool I love them, I meet my cousin Mamie Ruth Hamilton, After we put Zebedee in the ground I need to get home, Anger, Mr. Jones and Anger mother they was going to Pensacola, FL. I said that I can forget a ride, Jackie she had to work but her sister and Brenda they took me, to the Pensacola, FL. To the airport, Brenda she went inside the airport to check in, I huge Brenda I want to kiss Brenda but I better not, then I went to the gate to border the plane, I wait to the plane to arise, Then the plane came I got on the plane and took a seat.

I had to change the plane before to get to Vegas, after then the plane arise Robert and Joyce, they meet me at the plane, after

I got off the plane then I saw Joyce she call my name, I went to Joyce she said you had a good flite, I said yes it was good for with to go with it, she said it was ok, then I got into the vehicle then I spoke to Robert, then we left and went home, I call Jackie that I was at home, she said ok, then you got to some sleep you got to go work, I said talk to you soon, then I hung up the phone. I said will I do have 2 other brother for living, Mack Crosby and Clifford Bennett, I haft to get alone to myself, it is hard for me.

Then I call Mom. Evelyn she answer the phone, I said that I am at home now, Mom. Evelyn she said ok sweet she would talk to her later, I said ok then we hung up the phone.

Diamond, little Diamond it almost for her Birthday, I dint know what to buy, I was thinking to give my God Daughter, then I said that I would give her money, then she could buy anything she need, I gave her $25.00 and a card to give her mother Michelle Dupree, her mother Rita Dupree. I gave Rita to give Michelle to give her little Diamond, for her Birthday is 10-10, then I said now I got that away now I was Christmas time.

We walk around about 1 and half time then I had to sit down, and watch the Traffic to go by, after Oliver he come in the gate, I said there is Oliver now, Oliver he wave then he park he unlock the office door, then Charlotte she come in to make the Coffee, after the Coffee is made then Charlotte she motion, to come on to Coffee ready, then we go to get some Coffee, it is John (probe) and I drink Coffee, Alonzo he have hot Chocolate, we drink about 2 cups Coffee then I go home, or we stay out to talk, then I said it is ready for the Price of write, then left for home, after I see my soaps the news then I went to get my mail, I went back home and in the computer writing my book, I don't have no life but writing my book, Passing Through about my life.

Then I lay around sleeping, eat, writing in my book, sit around then I go back to sleep, go to the bath room, go back to bed sleep, go to the bath room then I get my push up it is 26 times, then I say my Prayer eat turn on my computer. Then I start walking around 1and half time, sit down to watch the Traffic, John, Alonzo, Cleave, Mary Helen, Mr. Charli and I sometime Robert, Mary Helen, Mr. Charli and Robert take the bus going to the center, sit around until we take the bus back about 2 pm. But we are retired we can do this, I love it.

The morning time I saw mom. Evelyn she was going to put her garbage out, I said mom. Let me take that, she said no son she need to walk, I said ok but I had eyes on her to see that she was ok, mom. She took the garbage to put in the depose, then mom to get her mail she came out, to say the peoples high then she said see you son, then she went to building 4 she living, then I was re leave then I went to some more coffee, and came back we sit around talking to John he said that, he was going to see the game, Alonzo he ask what game? John the lady game the William sister tennis.

Alonzo he said that he don't know anything about tennis, I said that I don't know anything I am going to the prize write, then I left going home, because that all I do walk around 1 and half time, then I look at the Traffic, and then Oliver he unlock the office, Charlotte she make some coffee, pat, Loraine and Charlotte she call us, then we sit around drink coffee, all the time I do.

It was November almost going it is almost Christmas time, I said that Little Diamond and IEJAAH MY God daughter, I got to save them $25.00 for each for them for Christmas time, then IEJAAH her birthday I after to give her $25.00 to her, Alonzo he said that they is rich, I said hum. I had a doctor appointment it was at 12-20-12 at 9: am. I went to the doctor he said that you are doing find, and come back to 3 month and he want to give some blood be four the next appointment, I said that think you doctor then I wait until the appointment and they give the blood form, then I went to my truck then I left.

Then Christmas time Michelle she want to un rap they present, to see with the kids IEJAAH and Diamond I don't care by me, but sometime they not to be able to see if they like it, I love anything to IEJAAH or Diamond from me. I saw Rita and Perl I said marry Christmas, I saw Cleave, John, Alonzo, Mary Helen, Pat, Charlotte, and mom. Evelyn I call her all to marry Christmas, I saw Miss. Russell, and Shrill I said merry Christmas, then I went home because It was Christmas time is not, as I was 8 year old I dint now that no Santa Claus.

CHAPTER 3

When I call John and Linda Marshall to say merry Christmas, I talk for a little while then I hung up the phone, then I call Angela and Mr. Jones to say merry Christmas, then we talk a little while then we hung up the phone, I call Becky to the kids to merry Christmas we talk to a little while, then Mary Carol BRYER in Brewton, Alabama to say merry Christmas we talk for a little while, I call Jackie my Daughter and her family, then I call my sister and her family, I said now I call everyone to say merry Christmas, then I put on my Computer to all to merry Christmas, for all the world to see.

It was so many Christmas cards, I think for everyone who was sent a card for Christmas, I would thank you for all you, I said the new year is coming, the last year she could be the better then her new year, I hope it is up soon, then I haft to get a regulation and keep it, it is new year eve I call Dense Smith in Chicago, I talk to her I dint call Robert I dint know his phone number, Denise she said the new year eve what you doing to the new year, I said Nothing at all, Denise she said if she was in Las Vegas she would find something to do, I said ok come on, Denise she said not then she said that if she see Robert she would tell him, I said ok then we hang up the phone.

Then it was new year eve, that evening at the night came the fire cracker they was lien up the sky, I said that the new year is coming but it was over. The 1-1-13 on ever the 3rd we haft to pay rent, I went to the Walmart to get a money order to pay my rent, I wrote the money order then I put into the mail slot, they would get it. 1-4-13 Gerald he use my truck to move something, after he brought the truck back I dint think about it, after I got in my truck I saw the upward at to the sun blinder, it was tore or tear I went to the office to confront him.

To face to face we went to the truck he saw the tear he denial it he was lying, but if he want to use my truck I would say no. January 18th 2013 Angelia Jones my niece, she was at the Reo. Hotel I took Mr. Brown he and I went to the Reo. Hotel to see my niece, I saw her we ate and we talk until Mr. Brown they took our picture to show my daughter Jackie, I saw my uncle David lee in Las Vegas, then Mr. Brown I we left going home.

Then I mail 2 books it cost $3.31 each to mail 2 1b. 6.00 OZ to mail to my niece Angelia, it was on January the 22-2013 Angelia she call that she got the books, she said that she will call in 2 weeks, I said ok. Then my God daughter IEJAAH her birthday, her birthday date is 2-11 I gave her $25.00 to buy something for herself.

June the 5th my birthday John and Linda Marshall, they call that happy birthday. John he ask what are you doing for my birthday, I said nothing it is only nothing day I am a little older, John he said may do something, I said hum then we hung up the phone. Then Becky she call to say happy birthday, she ask me the same as John, I said that same thing nothing, I hung up the phone Becky she was at work, then

Jackie she call we talk she had to go to work, I said go to sleep then I hung up the phone, Then Angelia she call me happy birthday we talk for a little while, then we hung up the phone. Diamond, IEJAAH and Michelle they came to my present then they left, then from: Louise Shell family we love you, then for mom. I wish you the best always thanks for all you have done for me, love mom. Then Robert and Joyce Thomas she gave me 2 Ticket, for the Spinners at the Cannery casino, I went I had a good time then I went back home.

The Father day June the 16th I had a card from Robert and Joyce Thomas, with warmest wishes on Farther day and a reminder that you're someone very special every day of the year! Enjoy your day. From: Diamond, IEJAAH and Michelle you're always dressed to impress, wearing your Sunday's best, may God continue to bless you today and always, happy Father's day.

Angelia and Mr. Jones, dear Uncle I love wish you and Beautiful Father day love your niece. Uncle David lee Father day, Father day is a nice occasion to keep in touch, and let you know you're thought about often-and wished the best always. Love always Mr. Jones and Angelia. Then John and Linda they call to happy Father day we hung up the phone, then little Diamond birthday on 10-10 I gave her $25.00 for her birthday, to buy something for herself.

My sister-in-law Annie Pearl Bennett she is in the Hospital, her Husband Clifford in Huston, TEX. My brother, I keep Pearl Health when she is feeling bad, I call him when she is to see how she doing, Clifford he would say Pearl is at home, I said see how she was doing, he call her to the phone she got on the phone, I talk for a while Pearl she said she was tired, I said what is the matter, she said her heart. I said cant they fix it, the Doctor said no she was tired, she said God was going to fix it.

Then she said that she was feeling bad, then she call Clifford he dint answer, she is outside, I said that I would talk to him later then we hung up the phone, I said Pearl she doing to give up I will send a pray for her, then Deloise Hill my sister call that Pass. I only get fix income and I sent money to the book 3 I ask Deloise you are going, Deloise she said yes and she haft to pay for Wander fair my niece, she is not work, I said when you get obituary for me, Deloise she said ok then we said I love you she said I love you, then we hung up the phone.

After the Funeral was over Eddie STALLWORTH he call me, Eddie he said here is your brother, Clifford he got on the phone, I said I was so sorrow that I could not to get to Pearl Funeral I dint have no money, Clifford he said she was put Pearl in the ground, we talk awhile then I got on the phone to Deloise, she said Pearl she looking so nice they put away so nice, then Eddie Deloise she said that he is the phone she would talk later, then we hung the phone up.

Home going Celebration
For Annie Pearl Bennett
Sunrise February 28, 1938—sunset September 6, 2013
Services Wednesday September 11, 2013

Viewing—9 A. M. to 11 A.M. service—11 A. M. Rev. Archie Thompson, SR.—pastor—My Mother was my queen. I have one Chair in my home. When she would com. Visit, everyone that was her throne! My Mother was a giver. She would buy all of the Chicken that was at Brookshire—not only for me—but for all of my Friends. She will never be forgotten—I still find myself looking forward to our good morning. My comfort is that she won't have to wake up sick and worry about me. She is moving Mountain. She taught us to pray and make sure that we knew that God was First!

It is little Diamond it is her birthday again 10-10, someone said that those girls love them, I said yes, and if someone misuse them I would haft to come by me, then it was Diamond birthday again, I gave her $25.00 for to buy something for herself. Then another Christmas time is coming up again, then Anger she call she said uncle David lee how are you, I said that I am doing find, then I ask what are your birthday, she told me, I wrote it down for until to use it, we talk for a while Anger she just call to say how I was doing, I said that I am doing find, then we hung up the phone.

Then I sent Anger, Diamond and IEJAAH A card and $25.00 for each of them for Christmas time. Then New Year 1-1-2014 I dint go out for the New year. Then the next mount Anger it was her birthday, I sent her a card and $25.00 for her birthday.

2-19-14 Mr. President. They say that you don't have the approve the score high, those peoples they try to keep you down, Mr. President keep up what you are doing, the Republican party they are hum, hum bug, because you are black.

2-21-14 Heaven and hell right on Earth. It not up in the sky if man he would saw it. Hell down in Earth now man they would found it. They put in the body in the ground or grave, they cover it up then they leave. Heaven, rightful, fair, just lawful claim rightful, ness love, Affection, passion ate of person for another or animal, this is heaven right on Earth, happy while you living, when you die. I don't where your Spirit go.

2-21-14 Hell, the state or place of total and final separation from God and so of ETERAL misery and suffering, Arrived at by those who die unrepentant in grave sin, any place or condition of evil, pain, etc. Catch or get hell slang to receive a scolding, punishment, etc.

2-25-14 Yes, I want a lady but, I don't want any lady or woman, I want to be Special. I will know how she handle herself, if I can have a lady to have she haft to be fun, but if a woman just to go to bed and put her cloth on, and pay her and leave, I don't need a woman don't broad me, if I can do bad along buy myself, I am going to keep that marriage woman?

3-13 14 Ruby, (KEE, KEE) Winter and her sister, I am looking for my Daughter Ruby and her sister, If they see them one are both call me my dad David l. Marshall 702-534-0839 call anytime.

4-2-14 my first wife Barbara Jean mother, to John Marshall. She has Cancer. Pray for her she is in Maywood, Ill. She is in the Hospital pray for all of peoples who Cancer, all over the world, Cancer is the number killer.

John Marshall he call that Barbara Jean she pass, I could not go to the Funeral because, I just go another book to pay for them, I dint have the money. Barbara Jean McFarland she had gotten that marry to a nothing man.

Celebrating the Home going of

Sunrise June 18, 1943   Sunset April 5, 2014

Barbara Jean McFarland

Tuesday April 15, 2014 Visitation: 10: A.M. Service: 11: A.M.

Wallace Broadview Funeral Home Funeral Home 2020 West Roosevelt Road Broadview, Illinois 60155 Reverend Theodore Matthews, Officiating

Obituary

Barbara Jean McFarland was born to the late David Stallworth Sr. and Lois Mallard on June 18, 1943 in Brewton, Alabama. Barbara received Christ at an early age at Piney Grove Baptist Church in Brewton, Alabama. She received her education at Booker T. and Southern Normal School in Alabama.

Barbara married her childhood friend, David Lee Marshall Sr. to this union two children were born, John Wesley and the late David Lee Marshall Jr.

Barbara relocated to Chicago, Illinois in 1961. She met and married Milton McFarland. To this union, Milton II and Yvette McFarland (Wright) were born.

Barbara was a very dedicated and hard worker at Borg Warner Automotive for 36 years. She retired in 2006. Barbara was known for her famous home cooking and her southern hospitality. She was a mother to many and a friend to all.

Barbara departed this life on April 5, 2014. She was preceded in death by her son, David Lee Marshall Jr. and her siblings, Robert (her twin), Christine, Rhonda, Frank and Carl.

Barbara leaves to cherish her memory: her loving children, John (Linda), Milton, Yvette (Timothy); grandchildren, John Jr, David Lee 111, Brittani, Keladrick, Nathanial, Diamond, Amya, Tia, Timothy Jr. Trevon, Miracle, Mya, Janiya, Barbara, Daniel and Jeff Jr. eleven great' grandchildren; siblings, Gloria (Joseph), Joi, Joanna, Andrea, Leon, Steven and David (Cheryl); sister-in-law, Mary; special daughters, Donnita (Phil), Carolyn, Mary, Victoria, Danielle, Mona, Javette, Kimberly and Anita; best friend, Francis Harris, and a host of special nieces, nephews, uncles, aunts, cousins and friends.

Happy Mother Day, my mother she pass on, but my Daughters and my Daughters in-law and my nieces, I wish to Happy Mother Day, and all wish to say Happy Mother Day to all. On 6-3-14 I wish Happy Birthday to me. 6-5-1942 I am 72 years, I want to get older, I wish.

God he is good he gave his only son. I know Jesus, I know what he are looking for himself and others. I know Jesus. Jesus first he was a mortal, he fell and hurt. I know Jesus. They nail him to a cross, and though rock at him until he laid him to rest. I know Jesus, how he passing through to touch each one. I know Jesus do you know him, he said coming back, he is good.

Take a look at yourself, you are gorgeous, fine, God he made you and them, God he don't put on the earth until you are gorgeous or fine as I am, God he made me. I may don't as other look as good I, but God he made me, I am looking good, I want to do something to help someone else, no matter who, I want to help someone be four our I pass on. I don't know what going on the other side. I don't care or whatever God he made the Devil too, God he is all Father.

You see I tried to just to see, I tried to forget God, I tried to forget him, but you can he is best a good friend, but God he is our Farther I forget him and I love him. I tried to walk with in the shoes like God. I tried to relive or live with God. I am he was a God the first son the Devil, Jesus I am the second son, I am the third son. God he told me David you are struggle now, you are going to make it.

You are I see peoples lots of peoples, I don't see no race or religion just peoples, I don't see no Black peoples, no white peoples, red peoples or what color they are just peoples. When I wrote Passing Through, God he gave me to, I was going name once and child now I am a man. I put it down on paper, I went back to bed, I tried to go back to sleep, I was working night, but I could not sleep I got up and took my paper, after I wrote Passing Through.

Passing Through about my life. I want stop because it is my life, God only stop my life only Death. I Though that I could to write about my life, if they the Family they want to read about my life, the money I don't care about that, I was necked born first, when I pass then I ware half suit, ever one of my family should purchase, one of my book call 702-534-0839 book one-book too-book three thank to my family.

God, he dint bring me far to abandon me, God he love us all he love us because how I we know all mistake we made, I made problem I ask my Father God to forgive me, to do something that I should not. You are going to die soon or later, o yes you better get ready because, the child Born to a woman going to get ready, we are going to die. Now after that I don't know but, you are going to die.

You see I been going to my eyes Doctor, sense about 2 years going to the eye Doctor, so the Doctor they said that, was you ready to be operate to my eye, I said yes! Ok it is ready then the nurse they are going to get a date, to operate for my eye, so the nurse got a date for 9-29-14 it was going to the right eye, date of surgery was Stone Creek 5915 south Rainbow Blvd. Ste. 108—arrive time is 7: am. Then after the next morning I had to go to Gold Ring office 9: 30 am to follow up, then I had to same office the at 11: am to the next follow up, then the next follow up 10-7-14 then the next follow up 10-20-14 at 11:15 am.

Robert and Joyce Thomas, they was with me they stay with me until the operate was over, until I got home then I got out from the vehicle, I said that I would see them, they said ok, then I said I love them, they said ok we love you to.

CHAPTER 4

*N*ow I know my brother Mack G. Crosby he was in the hospital, but he was not bad condition Deloise Hill my sister, I call her once a week to see how the family was doing, then she call me that Mack he pass on, I was devastate that he pass on I dent say good'bye, I call Joyce Thomas my cousin to tell Mack her cousin he pass, Then Joyce she ask was you going to the funeral, I said that yes get my ticket, I got enough money to pay for my ticket.

Joyce she got my ticket but I dint know that I was going around to Denver, CO to Chicago, Ill. My flight was with FLYFRONTIER. COM. But she got my ticket I went to Chicago, Ill. That I meet Clifford my other brother Daughter Felicia, I was in the Air Port they was looking for me, I saw her she look like her Annie Pearl Bennett her mother, I star to smile, Wander Hill they was on the phone Wander she must said did he see him, Felicia she said yes she got him.

Felicia she induce herself she said my name Felicia, I said I am my name is David l. Marshall, she said how was the flight, I said it was ok, then we saw Wander Hill she said uncle how was the flight, it was ok then we left going to Deloise house but we stop to purchase my Lottery ticket, then we went to Deloise home.

After we got to Deloise house we went into the house I hug her, Wander she said here is your room, I said ok then we sit around talking Wander Hill she said, why don't you call John Marshall he want to go to his house, why don't we are surprise them, then Felicia she said need to go to the motor bike bicycle shop, we left going to the bike shop, after then we got to the bike shop we look around Felicia she brought something then we left going to John house in Bartlett, Ill.

After we final got to John house we went into his house John he said pop you made it, then he hug me then Linda she was not home she had to work, but her brothers they was in the house, I spoke to them I sit down on the couch, then John he said you are all starving, Felicia she said yes, John he call for some food it was in a tavern.

When John he said let's go to get the food, we was John, Wander, Felicia and myself we went to the tavern, it was crower John he know the Bartender it was a white woman, we had 3 drinks and had some food, then we left going back to John house, I saw Linda I hug her we talk then I saw Little Pall, I said Little Pall how you doing, he dint know me, John he said that is my dad, I took him and I explain that when the Grandmother and John they was getting marry to renew they viol, I was the best man Little Pall he start smiling then he knew then, then he knew how I was one of Grand pow.

Then I went to sleep. After I woke up they went out and Wander she was on the couch, and Felicia she was on Air couch, they all was sleeping. I woke Wander Hill and Felicia I said we should get up to leave because, we got to the wake, we woke up John that we was leave because the wake, John he said that he had a ride, I said don't sweat it because it was my brother, so we left going to the wake.

After we got home Deloise she was dress, I said that I was going with that was I had on, we Deloise, Felicia and I went to the funeral home to the wake, Rickie, Felicia she drove to the vehicle for Rickie, we went into the funeral home I saw Kathy my brother Daughter, I spoke to her I saw Wanda I was going to speak to her brother Daughter, then she turn her head as like she don't to speak to him, I went to see the body, no one was in the funeral home but Deloise, Felicia and I, Kathy, and Wanda. We sit about 45min. Then we left I said Kathy she spoke Wanda she turn her head, I said that she I did not anything to her, I said well that was her.

That morning we got up and got dress to the funeral, Deloise, Felicia, Eddie Jose he pass Daughter her niece and I went to the funeral home, I saw Peat my nephew, Josephine my niece, Carline my niece we was talking, then Deloise she was in a wheelchair, I wheelchair and park at the first row, there was a good friend of Deloise she sat down I meet her, Felicia she park by close to get to ease to the wheelchair, Then we sit down Glendora Harris my niece, she was the preacher she said something I dint like it. But it was my Brother funeral I had to be cool, she said take out the trash, the hill family talking to Deloise Family.

After the funeral was trying to line up the cars for the grave site, we went far away to the grave site it was cold, cold, it was so cold Joyce she had some glove the lady glove, I dint put them on. I had on a summer suit, the wind it was blowing hard I said it not warm enough, Rickie he gave me a coat but to for that summer suit, I don't have any suit to warm it was in Las Vegas, I don't have a warm a suit enough I went to the vehicle, to keep me warm I look like a dog shit to simmer seed, after the funeral was over we was leave we dint go to repass we went home.

Later on Deloise and I was talking then my cell phone ring, it was my niece Addie she ask why dint go to the repass, I said that they was going home I had to go back home, I had to go with the flow, Addie she said ok then she hung up the phone, I said hum. Then Rickie my nephew he had cook some fish, we ate some fish Felicia she was on the phone.

Home going Celebration for Mack Glover Crosby Jr. sunrise April 3, 1937—sunset November 11, 2014

Monday, NOVEMER 17, 2014—Visitation: 10:00 A.M— Service: 11:00 A.M. Southwest Memorial Chapel

7901 South Komen sky Avenue Chicago, Illinois 60652— Apostle Dr. Glendora Harris, Officiating Mr. Lamar Allen, Musician—Life Reflections—Mack Glover Crosby Jr. was born on April 3rd, 1937 in Brewton, Alabama, to the union of Mack Glover Crosby Sr. and Ollie Lee Hawking. To this union three children were born of which Mack Jr. was the youngest. Mack graduated from Southern Normal High School in Brewton, Alabama, in 1956. He also graduated from the Chicago, police Academy and was a dedicated police Office for many years.

Mack was united in holy matrimony in 1956 to JERLENE Sanford of Brewton, Alabama. To this union was born two Daughters Wanda and Kathy.

Mack had extensive knowledge and passion for caring, training and racing horses. He love of horses led him to owning horses that took him to the winners circle many times. Mack was called home to glory on Tuesday, November 11, 2014—He leaves to cherish his memories: two Daughters, Wanda Howard and Kathy (Lindsay) SWINT: one sister, DeLores Hill: two brothers David Marshall and Clifford Bennett: five grandchildren, Michael, Leslie, Ashley, Aaron and Marcus: four great grandchildren: and a host of nieces, nephews, other relatives and friends.

Wander Hill she said we was going out to Gil's Lounge, I said that I would like to see him, I said ok what time, she said that she was going to sleep after she wake up. I said ok. After we and Wander we woke up we went to Gil's Lounge, we went inside Wander, Felicia and I went up to Gil's I said how was you doing, he was drunk he dint know I was, then I let him to know who I am I said the honey man, he said honey man how you are doing, I said this Wander, Felicia she came to TEX. Wander she was at here those nieces, they said hello, we came to my brother funeral to day Wander and Felicia they order some food, from Harold chicken next door they ask did something, I dint want anything.

Gil's he had the same thing begging you to buy him a drink, I said that I don't have any money, the beers $2.50 a bottle, the whisky cost $10.00 a shot, I dint come to Chicago to spend that kind of money, I don't drink anymore I hold that beer one beer until we talk to Gil's, Wander, Felicia got the food they was eating the food, then Pat his son he pass on, I said that I was so sorry to pat he is a good place.

Then Wander, Felicia and I we was going to another Lounge, all the crower was in Gil's Lounge they was dike, I said to Gil's we was leaving I said that I don't know how or when I was coming back, I said stay up until I get back, Gil's he said ok. Then we left I went to the bank to get some money, then we went to another Lounge on 67 and Ashland, it was full it had a band we had fun, after we got to leave it was snowing, then we went to the house.

Joyce Thomas she is so beautiful but, she made a bobo she had my ticket to for from come back, to Chicago, I had to change the plain to Denver, Co. to LAS VEGAS, NEV. Then Felicia she tried to change the flight, I said that to Felicia she said she was on the phone? But they dint have any luck. The next day Felicia she was leaving going back to TX. She had a doctor appt. Wander and I took her to the airport, I took her bag out the car it was my Clifford brother her Daughter why not, I wave her buy then she went to the plain, Wander and I left we got some lottery tickets then we went back to Delouse house.

The next day Wander she said Rickie he was going to take me to the plane, she had to work she said uncle she would see you then she hug me, I said ok don't work hard, she said nor then she left the house, Delouse and I was talking until Rickie he said you are ready to go, I got my bag then I hug Delouse she said I had a good time and the thank to stay with you, she said that was ok when you coming back, I said that I don't know then I left going to the airport.

After Rickie I said how much to take me to airport, he said nothing, I said thank I got out the vehicle he left, I had to take a bus to O hare I wait until the bus, then a nothing guy he said that I will tag with you he said ok we was talking, until the airport came finely I was lost the airport was hug, I ask for information they gave me information I was lost, you see if I don't know where I said ok thank you, until I took a trine someone else where are I, she take the stair up and until flight 761, I said thank, they said ok get off and go up stair you will see 761, I said thank you then I got off.

Until I saw 761 I got to the ticket line I said had to pay $25.00 the before to Boarding pass, I said that order a wheelchair then I wait until the wheelchair I got on, I went to a head of line they took my axe daily fragrance away they said it was big, I said you can take it but the other airline they let it go, I said it don't cost much I said hum. Then they took me to the gate to Boarding to plain. Then I was first on the plain then they took the wheelchair away, then we left.

After we arise at Denver, CO. They took me off the plain first to the plain, we was going to Las Vegas, NV. I said that I will not wait until I get to Las Vegas, NV. Then we lode to Las Vegas, we got to Las Vegas, NV. Then I was the first to get off they wheelchair me to the gate to pick me to Joyce Tomas, she call me I was on the outside I went to Joyce, she ask how your flight, I said is ok until I had to change the plain I was lost at O hare, she said she made a mistake she said sorry, then we went to vehicle I said hay Robert how you doing, Robert he said ok you though you was hunger we got some food, I said I was starve then I ate my food, then I said I got to the bank to get some money, to pay Joyce then I was going to home to call my sister Delouse, to let her that I was home, then I am going to bed, I did that all.

11-22-14 Zebedee the 4, I will be in North Carolina after the summer time, I was in Chicago, Ill. To barrier my other brother it was cold and the wind at the grave site, I dint have the warm enough to clothes I came to Las Vegas, I went to my niece vehicle to get warm it was cold, I thank you I appreciation to put the face book to put in the computer about my passing brother, thank you for the reader. I will let you to coming to North Carolina, tell Brenda hi. For me and tell her sisters and brother, mom and dad tell high also.

If I was down in out I could not help myself, I am going to ask my God Father to take me to home. Someone said you are at home, I said that, I am not at home.

11-25-14 If Bill Crosby, if anyone that the other woman that rap, that is not right woman they have feeling to say no. to sex pool woman they have feeling to right to say for sex.

12-11-14 My Loraine, I had a woman she got sick she almost got well, I was talking she said that, I interrupt her I said that I want her back? She was going with God. I dint say anymore but, I steel love her then I hug her, then I walk out the door, I said to myself if I would fight for my love, but God I don't mist around with God he is my Farther. I am one of son. I got to love him, I cannot mist around that, I haft to get another Lady or a woman, but any woman or a Lady.

12-11-14 If I can get lucky to have so much money, and you or I can to burn and you or I can have anything that you can have it, pay for it or with my signature. If you or I pass on and die money don't need any money, I am going up stair to be with my Lord. I don't want pain, worry, sorry, color I am going home with my Lord.

3-30-15 Name is David L. Marshall, my Father his name is Mack G. Crosby Sr. he marry to MRS. Ollie Crosby, the kids name Margieree Smith she pass on, Mack G. Crosby 11 they call Jr. he pass on, Delouse Hill, Delouse she had a son call Eddie Crosby he pass on, I meet one Eddie Crosby kids to Mack Crosby funeral, I don't know her I forget her, Eddie

Crosby his wife call Unicer Crosby she still living, call David L. Marshall in Las Vegas 702-534-0839

A body and mind is a powerful thing, the mind it make up to do anything, that you do anything make it good things or you can do bad things, taken money from kids mouth, because man he is slick, a good man he want do that, that is a punk loan money you or whatever to give it back. Don't say he don't haft to pay her back, she need to feed the kids.

4-2-15 Clifford Bennett my brother, he is sick. About time to pass on to be four the Lord, my sister Delouse she call me the other night about 6: pm, her Clifford Daughter Felicia she call her Wander that, she said that Clifford he was in the hospital, he starting talking to the dead, I said to Delouse that he was not talking to dead, Delouse she ask did you hear me, I dint say anything, then I said Clifford he was not talking to dead, he is talking to angel. Delouse she said that I love you then we be four hung up the phone, I said pray for him then we hung up the phone. I put in the computer to Clifford Bennett my brother in Huston, TX. Pray for him. Delouse call me that Clifford he pass on the Easter Sunday morning.

Delouse say are you going to the funeral, after the funeral for Mack I don't have any money, I only have fix income I ask Delouse are you going, she said yes but Wander she is not working she haft to pay for her, I said if you are going bring me Obituary, Delouse she will then we hung up the phone. Then Felicia she call to let me to say that Clifford your brother was pass on, I was so emotion I said my brother going I don't want no brother, then Felicia she hung up the phone.

4-7-15 When the dead body they are stiff hard to bend or move, they are going to a spirit, soul, (sense) ghost or angel go to God, after then I don't know!

4-27-15 At 7: am I got my left eye to operate on, to put a lens in the left eye. I did the right eye be four it was secede, keep my finger cross that the left eye will be alright, God is good.

4-27-15 I had to operate for my left eye, the doctor he said that to come back tomorrow to see him, to look at the left eye to see how it was coming, I said ok. The next day I went to the doctor office on 4-28-15 the doctor he check me, he said that I was doing find the operated was secede, I said God is good, Robert and Joyce I love them. 5-10-15 Happy Mother Day if you are not a Mother, then Happy Mother Day anyway.

After the funeral for my brother Clifford Bennett, Delouse she sent the Obituary it read, I said my brother was living good Daddy's Girl.

Home going Celebration for Clifford Bennett SR,

Sunrise September 4, 1938—Sunset April 5, 2015— Saturday April 11, 2015—viewing: 9 am—11 am—service: 11: 00 am—St. Paul Missionary Baptist Church—2516 Paul Quinn—HOUSTION, TX. 77091 713-686-6131—REV- ARCHIE THOMPSON, SR—PASTOR

Daddy's Girl, Daddy's Girl forever I'll be. Memories of times we shared will stay deep within me. Years of much advice, I cherish in my heart. I'll remember all of your words, although we are apart. As I continue to ride and start my life anew. I'll be your girl forever and forever I'll love you. Loving you always, Daddy's Girl

The life and legacy of Clifford Bennett Sr. Clifford Bennett, Sr. was born in Brewton, Alabama to late Andrew Bennett and LORRETTA Martin. Clifford accepted Jesus Christ as his Lord and Savior and was baptized at an early age. He was an active and faithful member of St. Paul Missionary Baptist Church. Clifford met Annie Pearl Lee and the two married on November 5, 1957. They were soul-mates for 56 years. Together they raised three children: Clifford, AUNDRA and Felicia.

Clifford was a dedicated husband, father, grandfather, brother and friend. Known for his charm and wit; he never met a stranger. His heart and home was always open. He is preceded in death by wife Annie Pearl Bennett, his parents Andrew Bennett and LORRETTA Martin, brothers Essie Mack Bennett, Curtis Bennett, and Mack Glover Crosby, Jr.

To cherish his memories, he is survived by his siblings—Delouse Hill and David Marshall. Children—Clifford Bennett Jr, AUNDRA SCURLOCK Rickey and Felicia Light, grandchildren—Christopher Light, Quinton Light, Rickey SCURLOCK 11, great grandchildren—Angelis Light, Liana Light, Aiden D. Moreno as well as a host of other relatives and friends. Rest in peace my brother.

5-15-15 I was watching Judge Faith, the other day about 9: am at 5-14-15 a preacher was on the t v, with a woman on talking about the other woman that he was sleeping with them, he change the tune he start talking about something else, the Judge she don't forget, the Judge she ask that what the sleeping with other peoples how many? He said about 3 others lady, the Judge she shake her head, I said you are telling a lie, the Judge she was telling a lie, I said he was telling a big lie if I would been in the ordinance If I was in the ordinance, that is why I don't go to Church, I use to go I joint the Church, I would gave a child to give the money, not all like the preacher the rest the of Preacher they going to tell a lie.

6-11-15 I went to the doctor the day, he check on my eyes both eyes, he told me that he don't have no diabetics, I reply no, the doctor he told me the number once more, the doctor once more time you don't have diabetic, I said God is good.

6-17-15 LeBron James, king James hum he call the best Basketball ever, don't say that the other can play Basketball Professional, they put 5 player and 10 player to make a team to player Basketball, who won Golden State Warriors the finals.

7-3-15 It is hot, hot, hot is so hot this summer ever, over 106-108-109-111-113-it is so hot as kind pepper.

7-17-15 Free, thing that does not exist for nothing for free, someone haft to pay. Someone else haft to pay the air is breathe in take into the Lungs are not free, the oxygen tank take someone need to breeze or breath into the lungs it's not free, someone else going to pay, someone they pay for them, then give them you that is free.

I was looking at the Sympathy card peoples gave and sing for me, that for my dead for Mack and Clifford. And Loraine her birthday party I went, and Loraine her Grandson Evie PEIRRE 11 Saturday Oct. 12 I could not attend but I gave him a present for the child, then Angela and Arthur I was looking and smile.

12-17-15 A man and a woman are nothing but a machine, to take care for our self, Maintenance to put on my health, some peoples I see that some had are have some body or one another put on a legs, arms, I had my both eyes to operation the doctor, he put a lens to see. I could not see the doctor was amaze it was secede, God he got control.

I forget to put into this it was my Birthday I want to put in, June the 5th Joyce Thomas she gave me some 2 ticket to the Spinner to the CAMERY to see the show for my Birthday. I said that I don't know who could go with me, I talk to John who I sit and drink some coffee, I ask him did you want to see Spinner at the CAMERY, he said yes ok he would go then he want the ticket, I said no I haft to keep the ticket.

I Though that he was going to go with me, until it was the show I got dress and I wait on John, and wait, wait and wait, then I went to my truck I went to building 5 I park my truck, I got out and went to knock on John door, I knock, I knock he came to the door, I said you are going with me, he said no he was sick and he said he not going. I got mad I said mother fuck you, then I left I got in my truck I was mad, then I said my cousin Joyce she got the ticket to see the show.

I would not go to waste them, I went to the CAMERY to see the Spinner, I ask for the lady I dint know them, I said my partner he could not go did they have a ticket I was going to give them, they said that they had a ticket, I went to the show the was crowed they was coming out, I had a white couple the next seats away, he said close my legs, I start to say something but I dint say anything, but after the show was over I left, going home I had fun I said thank you Joyce and Robert I love you all.

Rebecca Wagner I love her and the kids also, Joyce Thomas I love Joyce and Robert Thomas, Mike I love him also, these are family I love them always, I cannot get to in between them they both I love of all of them, why they cannot get alone, I pray for that to get alone.

Rebecca she call me once a month to see how the kids doing, Rebecca she work 2 jobs go to one then she go to another job, I know she are tried she told me, I told her that a woman she got to do what she can do to survive, I said go to rest go to bed I love you, Rebecca she said if I need something call me, I said I don't need anything, for you to get some rest talk to later.

Rebecca she said she said uncle David I will see you, then we hung up the phone, my niece Addie they cannot get along, I don't know how what, I know what they cannot get along, it don't make no sense.

Delouse my sister, why the family not talking, not speaking, to walking around turn their head why, the family is broken. You can fix it be four God and Jesus came, he is coming. Delouse she hardly can help herself, she is bent over in her back, Mack he has two Daughter why not take care for him, Wander or Rickey they want take care for him, why he had two Daughter Wanda and Kathy, so why Delouse, Wander or Rickey he could not take care for him, I was my Brother to, Bear the hatch.

A bully one day I was sitting out in the sitting area, I thank that I was a pussy because I don't talk so much, he was drunk he was drinking, he said you want a drink, I said no thank you, he talk about me lack he I was a dog, he talk to so bad, I said here it is now he was drunk, the management of Louse Shell name Gerald Jackson, he said that if anyone mist with me he said come in the office and let him know, I said ok. I shook my head he talk so bad he said that he said he would kill me.

I said ok I was going to let Gerald know because, I want get no trouble. After I saw Gerald he came in the gate and park, he went to the office, I said hello, Gerald he said high come on in the office, we close the door I told Gerald the secession I said that I don't want no trouble but, if you cannot stop him I would. Gerald he said that he was going to talk to him, because they had some problem with him, I said ok then I went out the office.

After Gerald he had a talk with the bully, he said to me he said talk with the bully he said that David he don't want no trouble, but David he was no pussy don't mess with him, you better not mess with him. Gerald he said he put something on his mind, I said ok think you Gerald, he said no problem he said don't have like the Indian, I said hum, every time when I see him he just look, I said that is all you look but you don't mess with me.

Then the Africa he start to fucking with me, I said please don't fuck with me I don't mess you anyone, because that I whip that Indian ass but it was over, the Africa he was drunk he was drinking, I had to talk to Gerald a gain, Oliver he saw it he said why don't go to next table and sit, and don't want no trouble because David he don't mess with no body. It was all the lady was out I said that bully are fucking with me, I had a talk to Gerald I said that Africa he don't say anything to me, I told him the same thing what the bully, I don't say anything to me, Gerald I must had something to say about that, because they don't say anything to me.

--------------------I am sorry that you doing--------if
I had bad I am sorry------if I had good I love you------the
Lady if I did some way to harm you-----I am so sorry please
forgive me—I am sorry.

Angelia BRYE Jones she got to Las Vegas to day 8-23-15 she
call me that she was at the Circle, circle, I call Alonzo if he
was going, he had a thing to do, he dint have anything to, I
will see you, I had something to do, but my niece Rebecca
she had a key, I went to the Circle, Circle, I call Angelia on
the phone, I said that I am at the elevator in the lobby.

She said that she was on the way, then I saw her we and I went
to meet we hug and her and I, then we went to take some
picture, going to get the picture we was talking, then we got
to the designate area to take the picture, we went outside then
we sit down on a bench. We took a picture it was nice, then
another one it was nice.

Then we had another guy could he take with my uncle
and I, he said sure we two picture we said think, he said no
problem then he went to work. Angelia she ask who the older,
I said out of 5 brothers and one sister to the BRYE family. 3
brothers with the Crosby family pass on.

Then Angelia she got on the phone to ZEB. Number 4 she
said he is in college, I said I know, then a picture in personal
I talk with him, I told him I love him then Angelia she said
that she was in Las Vegas, he said that he know, then we said
that we would talk to later, then we tried to get in tough to
get ZEB. The 3rd Angelia she said he was working, I ask he
must work night, she said yes, then we was going back to the
we saw another Lady she work in Circle, Circle, she Angelia
I induce her, Angelia she is so friendly, she ask how long

Angelia was staying, Angelia she said about Tuesday, the Lady she was off that 2 days, she had her baby going to school.

Then I gave the Lady my card to buy a book or books then we left, she got Mr. Jones on the phone then we had personal call, Angelia he had a tooth was out, she said why don't put in his tooth in, then he put in his tooth in then we talk, after we talk Mr. Jones then I was leaving to go home, Angelia she start crying, I said come on I put my arm to around and hug her.

I said come on let me see a smile, come on then she wipe her eyes, then she start to smile a little, then I said that was a good time then I left going home I found my truck. I was going out I got lost I was at the airport I said no way then, I stop and ask some information it was wrong way, I stop some more information it was wrong, then I got on the right way then I went home 3 hours to get home, but the God grace I got home.

Zebedee Brye   Dennice Crosby

David L. Marshall Sr.

Joyce Thomas and Addie, my neice

David Marshall and Addie, my niece

Arthur Jones and Angelia (my nephew and niece)

Caleb and Michelle

The Brye Family (My Family)

Little Sara, her mother and grandmother

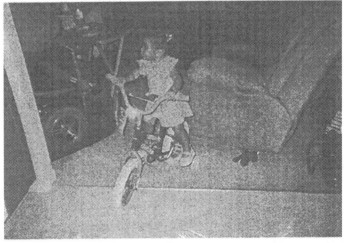

Little Sara

Devonte don't fall.

CJ and Devonte with a ball on his head.

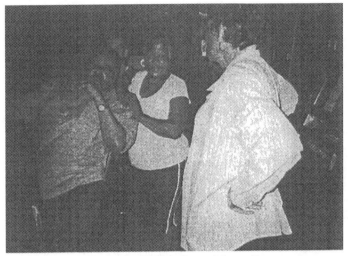

Big Frank, Bobby Offett and Pretty Pat

Becky and the kids

Linda, John W. Marshall and my granddaugther on of them.

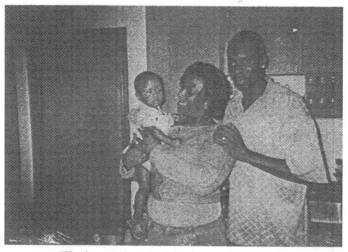

Wander my niece, Little Paul and John Marshall.

Pat another sister of mind, we was at a picnic on the park
67th Lomas

Ros, Josephine, my niece—Dor

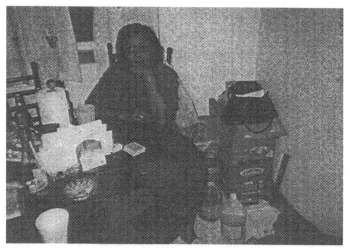

Barbara Jean my first wife.

David L. Marshall and Barbara Jean.

Eveat, Barbara Jean daugther

Robert for Weadwood Nursing Home.